Toward a Credo

Toward a Credo

Poems by

George Eklund

© 2025 George Eklund. All rights reserved.
This material may not be reproduced in any form, published,
reprinted, recorded, performed, broadcast,
rewritten, or redistributed without
the explicit permission of George Eklund.
All such actions are strictly prohibited by law.

Cover design by Shay Culligan
Cover image by Laura Eklund
Author photo by Laura Eklund

ISBN: 978-1-63980-709-3
Library of Congress Control Number: 2025933255

Kelsay Books
502 South 1040 East, A-119
American Fork, Utah 84003
Kelsaybooks.com

for Waylon, Thomas, Fiona, & Marina

Acknowledgments

I would like to thank the editors of the following journals in which these poems first appeared:

Eccolinguistics: "Tierra Humana"
Flare, the Flagler Review: "Marina," "Assemblage at the Edge of a Wine Glass"
Gravel: "A Long Island Sketch"
In Other Words: Merida: "A New Nation," "Before She Was a Planet," "Rivulets"
Lalitamba: "Clauses for Prison"
Literati Quarterly: "Escape from January"
Pebble Lake Review: "Essay in White"
Pegasus: "Essay on Two Hemispheres"
Plain Spoke: "1939"
Red Booth Review: "The Snow Is Wide"
Redactions: "Poema for a Lioness"
Reedy Branch Review: "A Song of Bare Trees"
Split Rock Review: "City by the Sea"
Storm Cellar: "Sketch in Early Fall"
Sun's Skeleton: "Anthem," "Third Martini in a New Century," "All History Is Mine"
Tinge: "Essay After the Twentieth Century"
Toad the Journal: "Sanctuary," "Motes of Orange," "Poema for Lawrence Welk"
Verse: "Pavane," "Bay of Stars"

Contents

A Song of Bare Trees	13
Sleeping Woman at a Window	14
The Opening	15
Composition on Mercy	16
Essay After the Twentieth Century	17
Toward a Credo	18
1939	19
Sanctuary	20
Motes of Orange	21
Poema for Lawrence Welk	22
City by the Sea	23
Sketch in Early Fall	25
A New Nation	26
Before She Was a Planet	27
Rivulets	28
Tierra Humana	30
Assemblage at the Edge of a Wine Glass	32
Marina	33
Anthem	34
Third Martini in the New Century	35
All History Is Mine	36
Laura in Lisbon	37
A Long Island Sketch	38
Poema for a Lioness	39
The Silent Riders	40
Essay on Two Hemispheres	41
In a Black Coat Beneath a Lemon Tree	42
Essay on Here and Far Away	43
The Silence When It Is Green	44
Essay on a Hair Cut	45
The Blue Trees of Louisville	46
Ten Robins	47

Essay on Rooms Where People Kneel	48
Seized in the Crossing	49
Nothing but Beautiful Work Today	50
Essay in White	51
To the Fourth Floor	52
Notes Along the Danube	53
Assemblage in the Last Snow	54
Assemblage in April	56
Always I Am Imagining Your Long Walk	57
In the Distance Between Papers	58
The Masterpiece	60
Essay in Early Summer	61
A Sketch by the Creek	62
Tempos and Temporaries	63
Purpurar	64
Poema Romantica	66
Poema de la Herida	67
A Red Kite	68
Late September Essay	69
The Elliptical Tide	70
The Pilgrims Move West	71
Awakening in the Shadow of a Roman Bridge	72
What Is Left	73
Pavane	74
Bay of Stars	75
The Snow Is Wide	76
A Thought	77
Clauses for Prison	78
Waiting for a Storm / Ready to Disappear	79
The Memory of a Cry	80

A Song of Bare Trees

The brain is the first subject
Then bring what you must into the mud pen.
I will walk toward the sun-lit grave
I will stutter with my baseball cards
And a rosary.

The brain is the first sacrifice
And there one lives
Or not at all.
For we are dropped into the virginal gasp
Of our impulse, afloat
In the upper realm of nerves
And the flurry of wings
We cannot see.

The morning star burns the eye,
A dead fly in a dream on a window sill.
The song of the bare trees
Holds the cold maze of the woods,
The darkness behind us
The darkness ahead
The melting ice within.

Sleeping Woman at a Window

How far did you go in your sleep
Gathering the elements of being
From blue flowers
Above the imagined sea
Always eating of itself
In the tempos of a death
Never realized.

How far did you go on the south train,
Sea wings glinting out of a vapor
Elements caught in the eye's atoms
Not far from the voice
Of a mother or a drum

Here is an open bottle and a clean glass.
You pick up a cloth, toss it
Upon a pile of stains.
In a mind lost above a noisy street
The jazz singer recites her lines
In Portuguese
A pigeon dancing at the edge
Of a spasm in a woman's eye.

No one can really count numbers
Or hear a song.
We put things in a line
But soon they disappear
In empty streets above the sea

Each cloud a monument
To the woman who sleeps at the window
Dreaming the next possible fragment
Made of stone.

The Opening

Tonight, she has been asked to speak
To strangers who may
Or may not appear.

They are making a movie of her dream
But it will never finish

To protect an hour
She keeps the eyes half closed

What is this art and this city
And why must she die.
When will the lover awaken
And why must she live

In this confused radiance
Amidst crowns and uniforms.

Composition on Mercy

Beneath the mask of a cloud
I rest my mind between continents,
Released into its fever where it cannot sleep.
Holding his ashes in a box,
Holding an absence emptied of light.
Death is always moving,
An apocalypse that comes and goes,
Something tired or wounded
Moving in the tall weeds.
I'd like to kill my face with soap.
An animal without eyes or snout.
Only a nova of muscle in a broken atmosphere.
The pores of the skin released
In a flurry of stars,
Magnetic tears set aflame.
Ornament without blood,
Some cold blue to fill the window
Above the asphalt lots that swell with fluid.
Music that means nothing
Except that I should buy it
And play it while I drown
Into the mechanics of mercy.

Essay After the Twentieth Century

The humans panic
When suddenly shaped by the beautiful storm
And the fields of gauze
A memory of a shave or some paintings
Or a walk through the poor district

To the eternity of an eyelash
Could you write a secret
In three words only

Watching the rain move in green
From the north across a grid that does not exist
I did not mind getting lost with you
The whales of the Atlantic were grateful
To have us whole and dreaming of them

The earth is ready to be done
With the last century
It seems the land knows little of itself
Erased by wind and water

But the new hour spins and the mind
Wants to know the voice
That held it all this time
And why it has remained.

Toward a Credo

I watch the gray waves of my face
And imagine the letters
I will never write.

What can I take
To help me see better
In my sleep?

An anthem is pulled apart
In the department
Of psychology.

My stomach dragged across
North America,
How does an acrobat dream

In the worthy patterns
Of a cripple
With holes in his shoes . . .

Gather some paper and mark it
And pass it around
And pass away.

1939

The dead soldiers dance out of the flames;
I kiss their fingers,
I'm not going in public fully for a while.

In the fast blades of the sun
A thousand eyes make a cloud
A thousand eyes in the rain
Beneath the wide colors of the flags.

The vine tightens in my throat,
A cradle fills with empty tubes.

I send the mind forth, waiting for a card
And a little bell to be dropped from a window.

Beneath it, my mother and her mother
Are strolling toward the park
Speaking of the World's Fair.
And for them, all birds seem mythological
And waiting to be born.

Sanctuary

Imagine a dead thing inside the sun.
What does it mean to be aboriginal?
Who is the new king of rabbits?

In a refinement of all that is Portuguese,
The garden is planted under the hidden eye.
Who could know if the work were imaginary.

She lived with him as a way to explain breathing.
They lived with a love of the high forms
Even as they renounced them.

They assembled their pieces of glass
around a dead thing in a cloud
And wrote their book in the sounds of Portuguese.

Motes of Orange

I have waited all day to go walking.
If I am not yet forgiven,
So be it.
I am learning to fear the moon again
And something of the planets within us.
I have to go walking
Toward my hidden name.

I have waited all day to be held
In the air as if I were a trumpet made of sand.
No one is coming for me at present
Though my killer may be driving aimlessly
The poor county roads
Held in a map of certainties
That neither of us can imagine.

For now, there is just an infected eye,
A hot compress as I wait
For the children of the yellow bus.
But the sun starts to winter itself
And the shot guns break the unknowing of the woods.

I wish my skull were bigger
And the torment made only of wind.
If I find myself walking at last
Through motes of orange
Then a color can eradicate
Even the specter of my killer,

His bad brakes, bald tires
And invisible, innocent grin.

Poema for Lawrence Welk

After the first sip, after the last sip
The North Americans come parading
Against this and that
Pulling one hundred and ten cornets in Styrofoam.

I am waiting for the swelling to recede,
Waiting for myself in an unsolved state,
Considering Lawrence Welk and all those pregnancies.

All of the God stuff makes its own sense;
People should relax
As honorable pigs, honorable loons
Singing for the spring ale

Walking the winter boardwalks
With a lover under one's arm
As if we knew Babylon

Or why reason shifts
Or why winter lights shatter
In the echoes of the snow

Where cars idle
Upon the darkening ice.

City by the Sea

The readers of old magazines
Can hear themselves breathe

In the cells of Lisbon
Nothing can be trivial.

Large plants grow dark roots
In the gut of the isthmus,

A soft pandemonium
Meant to save us, flowers
Brought to inertia.

In the seizures of the strand
The strollers have nothing
To say or offer to the empty faced

One feels lucky to feel the body
Pulled toward strange languages

The handshakes
In the midst of constant news,
In thoughts of the journey
Where birds were thrown toward the sea

A city filled with its last customers,
Children without memories.

One of them will scribble
The final sketch—
A picture of the big mouse
In my head

Who has never betrayed me
And whom no one can destroy.

Sketch in Early Fall

A list made of gray slabs of earth and sky
A dust made blue from the echo of a hidden tomb

Are you committed to amazement?
Would you like to drive to a museum?
And touch the edge of its stone corners?

The leaves are returning to me
All the small offices are darkening
The commute occurs in a strange hush
There seems to be no major theme

Perhaps the erosion of the air
That holds the veins

Has it always been a medieval life?
Did we ever fully escape the Baroque?

In a dream of rodents and religious medals
The swans were gliding away
Toward the preverbal

The sun cut by an oak tree
Children laughing downhill

A woman is putting on her costume
She will go dancing at the airport tonight
A man stares at a screen
Trying to remember Caravaggio.

In this brief time perhaps
We have kept a little of the world alive.

The castles in Spain take flight.
Every mother knows

There are words that can kill you.

A New Nation

A woman waits to fill with her own milk;
The practice of the world
Generates its dangerous frolic.

The darkness of violins moves
Up her arms and spine;
Not a trumpet is left.

The sound of brass is lost
In the winter stones
The earth will not release.

The hymns we sang
Ruptured in the winter sun.
Her chemical mind had no fear of time.

She was ready to join a nation
Of strangers where we would be known
And understood.

Before She Was a Planet

A globe enters the dream
And spins rain and missing
Faces wall to wall.

Children form
In a haze of bones.

The heavy breath
Of the blood trees pressing
Upon the glassy lake.

We don't want to believe in death;
It would mean the end
Of the imagination.

With a catheter slung
Over the back of a sterilized chair
I loved her before she was a planet.

Rivulets

Children climb a blue cliff
Into the fumes of the future.
They show allegiance to no one.

The church organist scratched his nose
And thirsted for a beer. He had traveled
To many planets

But no one knew.
Why is a nation beautiful to some?
How can a nation feel

Beautiful to itself?
Lovers try to love their dead language
In which they were told

A lot about their lives. Between rivulets
Moon to moon, people somewhere
Are chanting against old idioms of flight
Merging into blue

A woman stares at the night birds
Circling the head of the priest,
A Schumann symphony dissolving in her head
With the ringing
That killed the confused composer.

I am on the commuter train
To the prison, bringing my
Declaration of planets to no one,
A rehearsal in two parts day by day.

O micro-world of bricks, dark rooms,
Moving pictures,
Breaking the advertised image
A necessary sport,
A bleeding monument caged,
The hand covers the mouth
And is healed.

Body parts of the helmet men
Dance across the windows;
The rooster loves death.
The circus salutes loud color and gold.

Tierra Humana

A wanderer made of light reversing itself,
I may be hurt if I imagine the shore.
If my love laughs at me
I need not know the reason.
Which is more exhausting,
Religion, painting or love?
Air is air and making a question of me,
Making me into art
As I am air changing
In the momentary incline of an hour.

The wasp comes in a circuit
Where the girl child twirls;
Upon the blessed flesh
An aroma from the bog,
At the posts of the rich
The smell is the same.
Into a drum beat for slaves
Who can sleep?
At the door to the tomb
We must feed ourselves.

Don't send soldiers; send poetry
Cash and food.
The temperatures are scattered
So beautifully and unreasonably
Across the map, the earth's dream
Of itself as a god, a woman
Facing a death sentence.
A layering of medications in the sky.

A courageous smile is something
Nearly disgusting, watching one's limbs disappear.
Obnoxious laughter might be better,
A courageous grimace lost in a lake,
In a cracked day where the travelers
Are herded out to the street
For the long walk
To the border.

Assemblage at the Edge of a Wine Glass

At the edge of a wine glass
The owl blends the mathematics of the world.
My wife knows I lie because I am afraid.
The snow awakens a mother's belief.
When I love myself I have to laugh
And buy a ticket.
Silently as I climb, the crows must think
I am a hallucination that multiplies.
The world ignites itself and wants a God.
My dream breaks above the bathroom sink,
The hands betray the mind naturally,
Shadows worshipping faces made of glass.
The vein thrives, the evening pools,
The man's eye empties
Into something beyond himself.

Marina

She lay in bed waiting for everything,
She turned to the wall and saw
The shadow of a silent bell.

She did not need to speak
Beyond the shape she had become
Rising from the sheets.

Her eye already knew
Its own strange luck.
Her children slept in a naked

Ornithology composed for the future.
Broken jewels fell from her hand
In search of a tide,

A song lost in a cello
On the South Carolina coast.
She did not need to know
The reasons for the gifts we would bring.

Anthem

The moon lingered in the holly tree
Where a dreaming hand clipped a branch
And the silo burned beneath the neutered stars.
The Mexicans from Brentwood came down
To say a prayer.

A hidden mammal gave birth to twins
While the warships pivoted out of the harbor.
My spine darkened in the mouth of the fog
Where there are no shoes
And children are sent away
Inland to safety.

I drank a beer and thought of the insurance company
And nodded toward New Jersey,
One cold step knowing
How they extracted a god from the wreck,
The heart still beating in his head.

Most of what you hear through the day
Is a pop song or a report
And then your hands become more spotted.
As the world struggles to communicate
Its business, our only grace
Is to speak without purpose.

Third Martini in the New Century

With a mask and fast new wheels
Smoking at the dead station
The throat gone, the religious improvisation
Running I-95 down to Florida,
People watch the news for 28 minutes
Then collapse.

They work out on their skates in the beach towns.
We are all in the military air
Waiting for a car to leave or explode
In a crowd and a voice made of burned paper.

I miss my mother and her gin,
Her shopping sprees.
People are made so sick
They cannot speak or be touched,
So sick there is nothing
Random left in their brains.

A crust forms around the sirens
Of the low clouds and veins.
People form a knot in the public square
Without a plan.
Of a Monday and its public transport
Where would you like to awaken?

All History Is Mine

All history is mine
Though I do not want it blazing
Room to room upon each freezing wall.

The saturated field absorbs the slow dark
Of my mother's hair
Beneath the feet of invisible dancers.
Pale light holds the torn edge of a sound—
A layering of trumpets from the 1900s.
Thank God it's over.

The mind seems a blue fracture
Calling loved ones—how else to say it?
Bare branches and a face of leaves
Released into a list
Of every human I have known.

Laura in Lisbon

In a jet above Lisbon a child cries.
I am shirtless down below
In my sweat for you by the window
I am a biography of vapor
Carried to you in a brief melody
From the street;
Where do the endings go
When they are musing or incomplete.
I cannot smell myself,
I have disappeared in a long vowel
That no one can hold.

Now the wings above Lisbon are held
In the mouth of a psalm.
When will you release me
Back to the air?
You have inhaled my last
Molecule of thunder
And now you must decide
To be eternal in a wave or a wing,
A song or a cry
No one can remember.

A Long Island Sketch

The little boys and their wet bellies,
People want to talk about their beautiful families
People want to grill their meat
And converse and dip in the pool.

The little girls and their long dripping hair.
After five p.m. people
Want to talk about going to New York again
And seem glad to think about a meal.

The women realize again they are valuable.
The men realize again they are valuable
And though everyone has been hurt
And will be hurt

They can all afford a ticket
To some civil passageway
Where all can realize
How strange they are, irreplaceable

Difficult to reach
In hidden towns off the highway
Where there can be no cure
For their beautiful lives.

Poema for a Lioness

We fall asleep among the wounded,
We awaken in a flurry of moths

What cures can be found
In a kingdom of small wings
At the edge of a window
High above the colony

If you can hold the fine shape
Of a broken feather
You might find a neutral country

Children wandering a scattered field of nouns
Covered in roadside dust

You might awaken to a thesis of streets
Filled with an aroma you may choose

They tell the monsters
What they told them last century

Among the wounded in a circus of blood
We could meet a lioness
And press a shiny Canadian dime
Into her paw

A coin that turned up on a window sill
She would not think it strange
To be touched.

The Silent Riders

I have already gathered my stones
I only needed seven of them
In my wind-blown suit
I have a net in one hand
Along the impossible vein
The silent riders are moving
Toward the alabaster wall

How many names can the body
Call or hold

With swans, machines and medicines
What pilot could know
The necessary direction
Of a dream or bones in a storm

In the village of reptiles and rabbits
The warrens are flooded in whispers
Without mouths

No one can know my confession,
My abandoned wing
The names of the seven stones

The silent riders are made of plant and animal cells
They are nearing the alabaster wall
Awaiting a sentence
Connecting the butcher
To his lover's red hair.

Essay on Two Hemispheres

for Cy Twombly

Every nation bleeds beyond itself,
Shadows whistled in a barber's chair
Or in the emptiness of a huge bell
That hangs above a town.

I remember the last of my arrogance.
I wish I could have arrived there sooner.

After a great painter dies
There is nothing to say
And little to do but talk, drink
Perhaps stroll to a fountain.
The usual rejoinders want to be spoken
In an essay with veins to touch.

Out beyond the breakers some orchestral
Meandering brings itself to the edge
Of all art and war and famine.
The essential agitation.

In a Black Coat Beneath a Lemon Tree

In a sacred fulcrum of lead
The mind must follow
An avenue to a church as silent as a spine.
A weariness of flowers
A whistle for a dog
A stain on a couch
All waiting in a yellow vortex.
In the perfection of a leaf or a scream
Above the ocean surge
The mind is hard to sell or give.
It is held in rain
And caws out of its bird slaughter.
It snivels on a winter day
Across white hills no one can touch.
Across the desert of the lips
And the cold will of the window
Galleries of ash are heaped in a smile.
The age of the reptile is printed in a book,
and the pores of the face, a flurry of stars.

Essay on Here and Far Away

This window holds a scoop of light.
Behind it hides a slow genetic breakdown.
A card that says Congratulations
Tipped on its side.
The kids don't make puppet shows anymore.
And all the dogs are chained.
Someone sits here and far away in spasms
And here and far away the joints in the hand
Begin to throb.
They tear the face off a store and rename it.
There are exercises you can do to improve
Your shape and the way you think.
But blood and bone seem to know
Each direction is total.
There's always a bath to make the mind quiet
And buoy the nerves
As boys still roam the dusk in the steam
Looking for a place to dig a hole
For the hell of it
And call it an animal trap.
In the morning they won't be sure
Of where they were or who they are.
When they are old men
They will feel strange remembering
And knowing everything that needs to be known
When a shadow bangs the head
And a face lies stunned on a pillow.

The Silence When It Is Green

I have walked around many empty parks,
The emptiness feels the same.
It is a torture when the silence is green.
There is so little time to be alone and unsure,
The eye battered by the sea.
My bones are growing into a mist of faces,
For I am small and can only grow smaller
In dreams I cannot fill,
Held in the bones of a burning room
Where the lice survive.
The dead speak so fast in my head
Shadow to shadow, answer to answer
I cannot hold, driving them along the ocean
In my window glass
Or touching their arms in the sun
Between the bakery and the barbershop.
Under green awnings, the silence.
You could try repeating a good name
And imagine another earth in small breaths.
There is so little time for staring
Into what could never be done.
If I am really flesh, forgive me
The blood-stink of the hide
Forked out of a cirrus cloud,
A meaning to be laughed at, celebrated
And eaten when the silence is green.

Essay on a Hair Cut

I want you to cut my hair at least once
As a way to pray to the world
Against its ways which cannot change.
This morning the spider left an empty web across the door.
In the clay of my mouth a new nonsense forms
A creation that will not burn.
Cut my hair at strange angles;
I was born in a stadium of leaves
And pulled from the stones of an acropolis.
Make me rock-shaped and I may remember
My knowledge of the world's purpose.
It has to do with getting swallowed
At the library or on the beach in December.
It comes in a lunacy of rain on windows
Wondering how to escape the shape of the face.
How to speak to those children
No one can see
Crawling on my lap in their costumes.
I fear if I speak I'll frighten them away.
Shape me like the beautiful star—
The sky will be small and the sentences long between us,
The mind worked by the lungs and a lamp
Even as I am sore in the joints where the birds pecked all night.
Watch with me what walks out of myself and away.
Our nations are everywhere, though impossible to see.

The Blue Trees of Louisville

Driving at dusk in a blur
Of what we knew
The blue and bare trees of Louisville
Glide against the moon, the absurd sins
Of the beginning.
Clear thinking in certain ways
May throw you off balance
In the bare spaces between branches
Where I could draw and erase anything—
The chilled memory of a lamb.
If you're ugly and you disappear
No one will think about it for long.
Information keeps crossing my face;
Each night I want to arrive
In the arrows of the jet stream
As it rains beautiful rain
Through the dark of a thousand Spanish verbs
Repeating their future forms
In Louisville's bare blue trees.

Essay on a Hair Cut

I want you to cut my hair at least once
As a way to pray to the world
Against its ways which cannot change.
This morning the spider left an empty web across the door.
In the clay of my mouth a new nonsense forms
A creation that will not burn.
Cut my hair at strange angles;
I was born in a stadium of leaves
And pulled from the stones of an acropolis.
Make me rock-shaped and I may remember
My knowledge of the world's purpose.
It has to do with getting swallowed
At the library or on the beach in December.
It comes in a lunacy of rain on windows
Wondering how to escape the shape of the face.
How to speak to those children
No one can see
Crawling on my lap in their costumes.
I fear if I speak I'll frighten them away.
Shape me like the beautiful star—
The sky will be small and the sentences long between us,
The mind worked by the lungs and a lamp
Even as I am sore in the joints where the birds pecked all night.
Watch with me what walks out of myself and away.
Our nations are everywhere, though impossible to see.

The Blue Trees of Louisville

Driving at dusk in a blur
Of what we knew
The blue and bare trees of Louisville
Glide against the moon, the absurd sins
Of the beginning.
Clear thinking in certain ways
May throw you off balance
In the bare spaces between branches
Where I could draw and erase anything—
The chilled memory of a lamb.
If you're ugly and you disappear
No one will think about it for long.
Information keeps crossing my face;
Each night I want to arrive
In the arrows of the jet stream
As it rains beautiful rain
Through the dark of a thousand Spanish verbs
Repeating their future forms
In Louisville's bare blue trees.

Ten Robins

In a world that refuses to return
To itself, to know itself

Ten robins danced in a tree made of ice.

Awakening from pictures held
In the slow brain
We are the mystery egg, fertilized
In violent hope that a spirit
Might escape through us.

A woman collapses in a room
Above the desert, some green wing
Beating within her,
The memory of a shape in bed,
A wooden boat breaking in half
Floating away.

The body reappears in a little jar
At nightfall, the music so wide
It hurts to absorb.
Silence cannot easily exist
Except in the way of the winter sun

Preparing the eyes for a plague from heaven.

Essay on Rooms Where People Kneel

The icy light attached to the window
Turns the mind toward nameless yearning
In the dim tunes of the hound in the wind.

Empty shoes sit in a brain
Or fly across a room in the past.
Certain papers one cannot bear
To hold or examine
Except in a dream that does not arrive.

How the smell of the broken earth
Came into me as I sat
In my clean clothes by the window
And the smell of the clean sea
Came into my brain
As an instruction.

I wiped my knife upon a napkin
And opened to a frozen field I did not want to know
Where many plodded
In search of darkened houses
Sealed in icy glass

And rooms where people kneel and shudder
When touched by what they can't believe.

Seized in the Crossing

It is not easy for her to leave the imagined space,
To group numbers
Counting the times of instruments and methods.
A seizure of three deaths returns
In the elements that cannot be held.

In these hills people fear running water
And adore the spasmodic sun
As the hounds dream an old dream
That no one can think about.

Time lives in the formless rain
Waiting to be numbered,
Set in a table and forgotten.

Upon an altar made of lost sound
And limbs that tried to climb
Away from what the pharaoh knew,

Her whisper held in purple museums
Far from home.

Nothing but Beautiful Work Today

Take these eleven pencil nubs, I am through.
God is done being a meadow,
Done with what is written.
I was called by a succession of wrong names
And can never correct the body.
The mind kept going to the city.
You made a portrait of your face-
In yellow with purple lips and hair.
What were we called before we were born?
The eyes are burning but I have spent no money today.
Calling to the molecules of the unborn,
Nothing but beautiful work today
Squatting in the garden in the thick corn,
Pulling a tick from the nape of the neck.
Thirty dollars in the account,
This is an improvement.
While you were out driving
I kept learning the ways
Of what the mind multiplies
For no discernable reason.
If there are more words
It feels it has endured
Into something wide and blue
Or a piece of a window
We hammered into place above a valley.
I shall die with my hair long.
They called me a falcon before I was born.
The air is dense in the life of itself.
I could say something wrong about the light,
But the field floods within me.

Essay in White

A waterfall erased the faces, the rungs,
The crawling stomachs
Girls in white dresses moved slowly in line
To board the ferry that runs
Into a circle of itself
A white spider inched from a wrist
Through a dream
I nudged it with my nose
I scratched myself in limbo
And snapped the legs from a table
And threw them
Across the invisible floor
I would love to float toward your face
In my new canoe
Burning my plans for recovery,
My straw hair, my papered eyes
But the face sags above its decoy
In a lyric from any century
Shop keepers executed in the snow,
Their children asleep in the roots of trees,
At the bottom of a lake
In dreams of tobacco smoke
And white aprons.

To the Fourth Floor

Spooling and unspooling I am sweeping
The floor of the maze
From here to the octagonal sea.
Sooner or later a man must speak to the God of his mother.
You try to make yourself believable,
Knowable as a kite or horseshoe arcing
An impatient grace in the language of death.
The knees of little boys flash in the wide green yard.
Turned in my own prayer spreading wide in the throat.
To remember is to sleep
In a misshapen web strung from the hand to the mind.
Numbed or sanctified
Under the hand of the loyal boy.
As they wheel you toward surgery
Thirty violins intensify upon a single note,
A dog crawling out of the sun.
Find a cool rock that fits the hand.
Peel an orange over a day old newspaper.
Give away all your rings and drive,
The spine burning in its position.
Sit in a room and imagine yourself painting it.
Stand high above a river and listen as it freezes
In the snake head, the cow heart,
The fission of a star.

Notes Along the Danube

The spasm came, about the size
Of a quail's heart.
A green face in a Lenten shadow
Is always reading what I write,
What I take and carry
From the bags of children's leaves.
I look at my vein, waiting for it
At the surface.
Perhaps it will turn into a cloud
And disappear in the throat of a jay.
With the sun upon my mouth
Something must be growing
Out of my forehead, something yellow
In its new hour listening
Through small square rooms above a river.
The mind finds a wholeness
In what seeks to destroy it.
Along the Danube where I have not been
The arrival of night is worth everything.
An explanation rises in the mist,
A blue skimming stone
Thrown over and over again.

Assemblage in the Last Snow

In one more snow, an essay with no beginning,
Beware of the deity you feel within.
On a Tuesday in the orient
On a Thursday in the Netherlands
Beware of your face like water
Repeating itself around the knees
Of a man and his oxen—they are
Coming out of time and ambling
Toward the navy at Jacksonville.
Beware the dog at your feet.

In one more snow there are many places to hide.
Tell me what the dead are wearing.
I have found your eyes, your breasts
The sound of you in the electric surface
Where we went as children.
Tell me what the dead are thinking.

A stampede of shadows accelerates
Toward a harp dangling in my sleep.
There are so many locations remade in the brain,
The highway collapses in fog.
The madrigals are coming, like it or not.
They don't care that you have the look
Of a man in a financial meeting.
When they touch our flesh
We will acquire ten more names,
Ten more ways to forget.

Into the pulse of the flame
That ate all that paper
I burned on a hill,
If only a breeze could mean something.
I touched her after I burned her letters
And my whiskers turned gray.
There would be no symbols, no statuary.
Only lost men arriving
From new knowledge.

The music becomes very old again,
The snow breaks just an inch from a wing.
What would it mean to have a strong mind?
Beware of what you feed to the deity within.

Assemblage in April

Into the urge a stranger comes
Through baleful new born rays of blue.

Every narrative is a scrap,
The creeks are swollen eye to eye
In the puzzled hour of light.

A stray mammal has lost its teeth and fur,
I have washed the porch of excrement.

After several drinks at the airport
Only oblong desires for fruit
And mercy remain.

Always I Am Imagining Your Long Walk

A creek darkens in the window,
Is that the creek where you bled?
Trying to break what is unreal
Up in the woods above Bradley's hill

A deer came upon me once
And frightened me with my own face.
And then the sound of unattached bells
Over the town.

Tumors had started to bud
Upon the inner dark of the air.

In all of that sick moon
I could not sleep beneath the owls
Imagining your long walk to the creek.

Build a fire and wait for rain,
For the field to clear
Of hazy fliers
And all imaginary mammals.

In the Distance Between Papers

Into the history of coins and birds
Something wet and gray falls
From my body.
It is only 4 o'clock,
This sky could not be human.
Consider the crowd leaving the theatre
Hunched into the rain,
Minds lost in the distance between papers.

After a night of being shorn in their sleep
They are given a piece of fruit to hold
For a morning drive, old school songs
Dribbled from the mouths of the police
Who waved farewell.

I am held in something old,
The flash of the wing against my liver,
Some Egyptian shadow
Covering the hole in my hand.

How can that sky be a sky.
How could a bird be a god?
Consider the crowd and the bliss
They have heard about
Or watched from a distance.

A curled horizon handed to a prophet
On a morning drive
To the landing site in the desert.

Always I Am Imagining Your Long Walk

A creek darkens in the window,
Is that the creek where you bled?
Trying to break what is unreal
Up in the woods above Bradley's hill

A deer came upon me once
And frightened me with my own face.
And then the sound of unattached bells
Over the town.

Tumors had started to bud
Upon the inner dark of the air.

In all of that sick moon
I could not sleep beneath the owls
Imagining your long walk to the creek.

Build a fire and wait for rain,
For the field to clear
Of hazy fliers
And all imaginary mammals.

In the Distance Between Papers

Into the history of coins and birds
Something wet and gray falls
From my body.
It is only 4 o'clock,
This sky could not be human.
Consider the crowd leaving the theatre
Hunched into the rain,
Minds lost in the distance between papers.

After a night of being shorn in their sleep
They are given a piece of fruit to hold
For a morning drive, old school songs
Dribbled from the mouths of the police
Who waved farewell.

I am held in something old,
The flash of the wing against my liver,
Some Egyptian shadow
Covering the hole in my hand.

How can that sky be a sky.
How could a bird be a god?
Consider the crowd and the bliss
They have heard about
Or watched from a distance.

A curled horizon handed to a prophet
On a morning drive
To the landing site in the desert.

Something wet and gray
Is rising from the runway.
I am held in something new,
An oval drawn around my length and width.

Consider the crowd attending a birth
Forced to their knees
Under the weight of their parallels.

The Masterpiece

When I hold my chin briefly in my hands
I love the smell of soap before dinner,
The world starving around my twisted luck,
Breath making its own sense
In my wagon of gray light.
You will know what I am doing
When I hold my silence after dinner
In the smell of strawberries, coffee,
Polite talk draining down a tunnel
Or in the wake of a rocket.
This masterpiece, this recording of breath
As the angels mount their trampolines.
I want you to know what I am doing
Loving the smell of soap on my hands,
The fact I hold before and after dinner,
This masterpiece of the hurt world
That cannot feel itself, finish itself
And be known.

Essay in Early Summer

That my father wept
Each time a child was taken.
This life means waking under a shifting sky.
We ate and played as the day
Moved mind to mind.
Roll up your blue sleeves and be patient.
You can honor death by wearing rings and used clothes,
Holding an empty cage above the delta of our pledge.
The wasps have gone into their dark ways
And never see the moon.
We touch the rose muscles of late summer
And blood grows with what we planted.
We have no time to apprehend
A galaxy made warm in a book.
I want to speak from under your eyes and breasts,
The fans turning an idea of knowledge.
What is fervent is the first to die,
And the loveliest touch creates a disorder.
But the bones of my face are glowing
And cannot die enough
Though I weep with my father
From one sky to another.

A Sketch by the Creek

The boys bend and squat in the minnow pool.
The rain never came.
The boys keep growing the length of the creek,
Following their own knees and voices
In the warm July haze
They will barely remember.
I may have to tell them how evening came,
Leaving the storm somewhere else;
How many crawdads they caught that day
And it was their mother who showed them how.
No one can teach them how or what to remember.
I will stay close for as long as I can
To tell them it was or was not so—
Twelve crawdads they carried home in a blue evening.
And their mother showed them with a bucket and a stick.
On this, I make myself certain.

Tempos and Temporaries

Beneath a wide purple cloud
The dreamless sleep of mollusks
Hums in a green sea.
The song we cannot hear
Celebrates the wheel and the axe,
Mammalian fur and the hacksaw,
The mortician's wish and the ladybug.

How I shudder upon hearing
The ovarian whisper
The dialogic spasms
Between the throat and the hammer.

Carried away upon a schooner
Drumming with a teaspoon at five o'clock
I would like to walk the dune with you
And find a way to quiet myself.

I am the one who believes in the magic stick
And the trumpets of darkness,
Who wants to learn how not to read the news
Carrying a yellow flower to the grave of the sea.

Stop hating your mind
Stop burning things you cannot see.
Monsters are made of time
And the thorns of morning
And the rusted coils that connect us.

Purpurar

A man stood by his garden;
He was filling with time and weeks.
Rome flamed again
In apparitions made of twine.
He would have to get something removed
From his body but he knew not
What nor where it would be found.

A jet fumed in several directions of the vein.
A tomato plant began to shriek
Waiting for a shadow,
A man stood in his teachings and began
To bend in a cramp of dust
Beneath a beautiful red roof
That no one could see.

In the vegetation of a promise
Populations drove to bodies of water
Droning in tempos of a peculiar rain.
People began to fade and form
New nodules of sacred families
Recoiling from ideas of greatness.
A man came to believe

He would be an associate
For the rest of his life.
This seemed the last great idea,
Haunted by all of his errors
As elements of beauty.
He began to feel a lightness in the bones
That held the mind aloft.

There were no friends, only vessels
That ate history as leaves dropped
Into the low pools of the creek.
While a woman carried her children uphill,
The man did not know if he wanted
To follow or to hide.
When the ice came back in his beard
His country had gone to war again.

Poema Romantica

With a degree of repair in 17 countries
There are pictures of my face
Lying parallel to the sea,
Perpendicular to the sea,
The north of my brain has not been found.

Every dream is a purity remade.
The traffic spins toward the terrace.
Rain and suitcases on a corner,
Who has time to read?
We curl into our anti-narrative.
Do you recall your favorite photos
Taken against the brick.

As the city darkened and awakened
We came from the south by train.
Why should I remind you,
Have you not heard enough?
Must romance survive itself?
Love forms from confusion to confusion.

How can I ask you to remember anything?
I might touch your shoulders and find you
Turned into another creature no one could know.

When I drive it is especially dangerous.
The mind thinks itself free
And passengers keep appearing and disappearing
And my face lies in photographs of the sea.

Poema de la Herida

There is no other source of beauty than the wound . . .
—*J. Genet*

Faces of infants in the haze of Nicaragua,
Flights above history, a small engine
Fading into the core of August;
Any word can be made beautiful.

Consider the dream you had
Of wheat and plaster stars,
The insane guard of the tower
Who wept in his rainy wire.

Tell me the story of those blossoms
That are neither pink nor red,
Those deranged blossoms
That cannot die

Decorating the temple wall
Until it disappears.

A Red Kite

A bitter sap takes the nerve.
I watched my sons drive away.
The mind perceives what it cannot have,
Scrawling toward the sleeping town.

The mind gives back something hurtful.
The mind preserves a young girl
In her dancing steps.

Make it go away and it comes closer.
I am a fortunate man without destination;
I don't want to be drunk or sober.
Could the mind make itself disappear

Into a star or planet
The color of a jewel
Lit by distant headlights.

Children are running across a dark field.
In answer to a talking flame
Ghostly people kneel and wait
In turbans made of cellophane.

I keep leaving the many natures
Of my native land, followed
By an army of imaginary mice,

Shadowed by a red kite
That belongs nowhere
And the scars of a sleeping town.

Late September Essay

How perfect and how lost
The winged insect asleep
Against the dark glass

A plume in a jar
Something maroon to remember
And toss away

Into the bleachers
The moths dancing
There never was much control

On either side of the solstice
I want to go back to Lisboa

I pushed a button and there was blue
On my finger
I wanted to mutter, to hide

Look at how we have carved
This accidental geography.

The Elliptical Tide

The sea barked my name across the dinner table

I had been waiting all day for my hair to fall
Into the souls of the chickens

A perfect name is a perfect flood
When attached to the stomach

A word is a system
A protein, an ion, a flickering in the blood

When the meaning disappears
It is beautiful
Waiting for it to return

Purple archers are crawling through the field
Trying to kill a disease with their arrows

In the warbling of the future
All gazetteers will be buried and the one-legged man

Will be feared
As much as the three-legged man

And I will be following
Seven white hens
To the sea.

The Pilgrims Move West

When surrounded by something invisible
Anyone can become distorted.
Or people will form lines at ferry docks
Holding glassy eyed children
And blankets tied with string.
They disappear, awaiting the death
Of the king's stomach
Which they have never seen.

In the miracle of the brain,
In its lost fortunes
They await the coming of the ants
In a poor tailor's dream of the tropics.

Stripping oneself each night
It is easy to pull down
The many schools of art and government
With impossible conversations and rescues,
Baskets of fruit and dry blankets.

You are surrounded. Go ahead,
Hanging over the sink
As if you were a pilgrim,
Ready to be beaten
By mathematical love.

Awakening in the Shadow of a Roman Bridge

Held in the echo of a stone arch
How the fly slows its way toward my brain.
I do not know how to keep him or salute anything.
After blooming, the field
Is a memory of chaotic palaces and pleasures
Explaining the new rules of heaven,
The new rules for surrender.
You must hear a voice not your own,
Perhaps a voice released from the carcass of a fly.
We want to know heaven over and over
But it is not necessary.

Take my ring and take my note,
The streets are burning again
Through every civilization and revitalized forms
Of what is ugly, waiting for rebirth.
Take my ring and leave my essence
At the edge of your hand.
Take my stomach and hand it to the surgeon,
Take my shirt and wipe yourself.
Take my bell and throw it to the frozen river,
Take my skull and roll it across a summer lawn
Or give it away to the jewel thieves.
If there is a soul it is a vapor
Fanned by minuscule wings.

What Is Left

A man, a woman
Pen and paper in a room
Above the street where a dog
Scolds the drunks homeward.
A man, a woman
And their tickets and the crime
They have not committed.

What is left.
A woman silent in the tub.
When they broke their salt
There could be no diversions
Except for a glint of light
Upon the sound of a limb
Raised out of the water.

The risk is great, words
Disappearing in their rope work
Room to room.
What is left, a breeze
Without a season or a sound
Following them into the shadowed
Cathedral stone.

Upon the fine hair of their arms
Thunder, afternoon thunder
Made of light unseen.

Pavane

To endure the severe currents
Trapped in the brain
One needs a strange bird call
That comes only in sleep.
The mind wants to begin again in dark berries
But finds it difficult to un-know itself.
It takes a large poisonous bug
To keep my creature in its cage.
How far from your mind is the sea?
My mother cannot find rest anywhere.
I begin to collect parables of sand
And coins that once were Spanish.
The mind makes its phone calls to no one;
The orbit of the gray matter
Is difficult to escape.
My daughter made a dinosaur
Out of paper and tape.
The crows in their long history
Know the echo of an opera not yet written
And the bleeding mechanism
On the new Pope's head.

Bay of Stars

If the hands dehydrate
Something must have happened
In the dream of the mind.
O sacred head surrounded
By the crowns of rivers
And the loam of the dead
The silt of time
The ecclesiastical flow
Of the eddy pools
Where my brother liked to fish.
Tom, I like to imagine
You will come for me
And we might find ourselves
On a sunny incline
Overlooking the bay of stars
Crashed upon the waters.
What is the history of a nerve
What is the future of a nerve
We are given such sacred material
In these vaporized remains
Perhaps you could remember
A tree or a breast
And begin again.

The Snow Is Wide

My eyes are so small
When I touch them with my thumbs.
A glass of gin rotates 16 hours
There are many ways to move
From the shadows of thinking.

The dreams get stranger at midday—
Beautiful things distorted
In their new wreckage
And things I'd like to say.

I waited all day for the meteor,
The spitting snow electric,
The stuff on my desk held
In the silence of a maze

All day while waiting to die
I have wondered
How to put your breast in a sentence
In order to love you again
The mind is the slowest
Part of the world
To heal.

A Thought

Something blue flashed in the bare woods.
Perhaps it was a thought cut loose, set adrift
From the docks, the stone cliffs,
Some idea, some beautiful idea . . .
A piece of lint flicked
From a long dark coat once given
From a woman to a man to a man.
Some blue blotch left to float
In the bare branches of a long life,
Waiting for dream beats and a fire ring,
An old woman to tell the story of blueness,
An old man to sleep back and forth
As witness to the origin of beautiful thoughts
And how they are lost and left to float
Through a life and into bare woods
Filled with stars we will never find.

Clauses for Prison

A lone dog in the muddy field sniffs the ash
That floats from the creek.
Who sent the dog, who sent the ash?
Which words to take into a jail cell?
The lent of a mind, both axis and estuary
Breathes in a minor chord.
Friends send thoughts that cannot be held.
Asia sealed in a can of beer,
A loud machine moving in and around the intestines
I walk into a prayer
That can hold nothing except itself.

The speed of nothingness acquired in a crow's eye
And amusement of rockets in a park of wheels
And citizens screaming, in love with death for an instant.
Pulled across the desert of the surgical dream
Following my mother into the drone of the sun's ether
The face sags crookedly and becomes art
At the edge of the planet I created.

As the mouth approaches
Mammals turn in their sleep
And dream of hunters
Who want to love them
And make them feel strange,
Saved by one deadly arrow,
A bloody wreath hanging
Upon the height of the skull—
A motion of thieves rising from dinner,
A gathering of the things we cannot say.

Waiting for a Storm / Ready to Disappear

Anything massive can disappear.
Something green to hold, to be held by
When the body stops floating.
I am getting cleaner and more lost.
The bay is icy, the garden is bitter.
The bird of sun or shadow knows its way,
A red hawk gliding over Faye and Donnie's field.
A compulsion without a name,
A pathology without a mouth.
A damnation I could not see.
We would like to live as if we were not sick.
We want to bring someone with us
Following a gull flying low toward the city.
Sitting down to watch the last game
In little altars of stone
Who could construct a show about us
Tapping a foot upon the spinning earth.
Cultivating silence, I felt rich for a moment
Loving human loneliness.
The liquid stars must know so little,
Something kinetic and of no use.
I felt us begin to disappear
In those tunnels that carried us
Under a mountain and into West Virginia,
Into patches of light we cannot hold and cannot break.
I think I am a green immensity.
I will go upstairs and watch the storm
Hit the tops of the distant hills.
And I will eat it from my hand.

The Memory of a Cry

In a tired formation of shadow and wing
A sleepy sky
Ends in flat glass.

How might I know my own hand
As it touches that cloud
Or the hands of my children . . .

I cannot count well but I form
A word and feel its history,
The future in my mouth
Though it will soon escape
And hide in the room that faces the street
That circles my brain.

The day begins with a fresh, difficult thought,
The body burning a delicate darkness.
How the hours are rolled in seizures,
Myths shattered and remade
From what is shattered.

I have been reading a long book I cannot finish,
A book made from the ends of things.
Images burn the fingers;
I would like to lick them
And be done with myself

Where cracked marble slabs
Cover the memory of a cry
And the word it may have found
In the language it might yet make.

About the Author

George Eklund's poems are published widely in North American journals, including *The American Poetry Review, Beloit Poetry Journal, Crazyhorse, Cimarron Review, Epoch, The Iowa Review, The Massachusetts Review, New Ohio Review, The North American Review,* and *Willow Springs,* among others. Most recently, his poems have appeared in *Reedy Branch Review, Route 7, Rising Phoenix Review, The Lindenwood Review, Poetry Fix, Red Booth Review,* and *Rio Grande Review,* as well as *The Heartland Review, Descant, Redactions,* and *Adelaide.*

Eklund's full-length volumes include *The Island Blade* (ABZ Press, 2011) and *Each Breath I Cannot Hold* (Wind Publications, 2011). Finishing Line Press published his chapbook *Wanting to Be an Element* in 2012, as well as his recent collection, *Altar,* in September 2019.

His translations from Spanish have appeared in *The Rio Grande Review, In Translation/Third Rail, Merida Review, Circulo de Poesia,* and in the anthology *Sólo una vez aquí en la tierra: Cincuenta y dos poetas del mundo* (Only Once Here on Earth: 52 World Poets). His translations of poems by Mario Bojórquez recently appeared in *Tupelo Literary Review.*

Eklund has been recognized as an Al Smith Fellow by the Kentucky Arts Council. In 2014, he was invited to represent the U.S. at the Encuentro Internacional de Poesia in Mexico City where he was a featured reader.

George Eklund is Emeritus Professor at Morehead State University. He shares studio space with the painter and poet Laura Eklund on thirty acres of wooded hills in eastern Kentucky.

www.ingramcontent.com/pod-product-compliance
Lightning Source LLC
Chambersburg PA
CBHW031203160426
43193CB00008B/486